MY 1ST BOOK OF
COMMUNITY
SUPERHEROES

By Sara Kale

Amazon Page : amazon.com/author/rainbowartsstudio
Email : sara.rainbowartsstudio@gmail.com
IG : rainbow_artsstudio

What is a Community?

A Community or A Neighborhood is a place around us, where people live and interact with one another

Who are the
Community Superheroes?

Community Superheroes are people who help us stay healthy, happy, safe and connected in our neighborhood

Teacher

A Teacher helps
kids learn and educate
at school.

Mail Carrier

A Mail Carrier

helps deliver

mail to our home

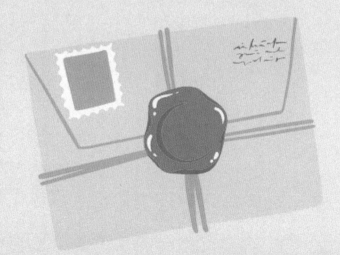

Librarian

A Librarian helps people use books, materials and resources in the library

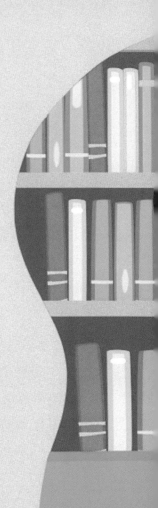

Garbage Collector

A Garbage Collector helps collect garbage from our homes and keep our community clean

Doctor

A Doctor helps cure people

when they are sick

and to live and stay healthy.

Nurse

A Nurse helps doctors take care of patients.

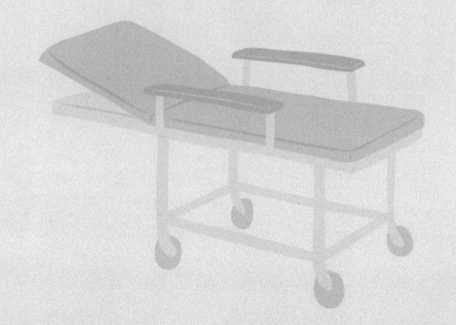

Police Officer

A Police Officer helps serve, protect people and keep our community safe

Firefighter

A Firefighter helps
put out fires and
teach us fire safety

Activities

Whose hands are these ?
Match the picture to the community hero

Mail Carrier

Garbage Collector

Doctor

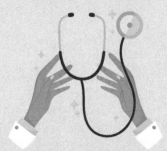

Fire Fighter

Made in the USA
Monee, IL
12 September 2024